A MOMENT IN...

Jenny's Day
2012

Comic strip, Self-Journal, Family, Stories

Jennifer Estrada

Jennifer Estrada

The following document and illustrations are copyrighted, © by Jennifer Estrada. All Rights Reserved. Reproduction of any part of this work, mechanically or electronically, beyond that permitted in Section 107 or 108 of the 1976 United States Copyright Act is unlawful without the expressed written permission of the copyright author and publisher.

Publishing Service

www.alphaacademicpress.com

Copyright © 2012 Jennifer Estrada

All rights reserved.

ISBN-13::978-1470074708
Title ID: 3797947

Jenny's Day

FORWARD BY THE AUTHOR

Welcome to Jenny's day. This book is my first in a series, and the result of the debut of my blog that I started back in the Fall of 2011. It sure was a crazy time in my life. I was working and raising a family. The children were in the ages ranging from 1 to 14 years. I was trying to find a way to finish college, and in the midst of it all, moving into a new home, which we hoped to get done before the Holidays.

My hopes were to turn my blog into a snip-it journal of drawings and stories that would let you take a glimpse into the life of a working class family, my family, doing everything they can in a struggling economy. And maybe when you read it you will see the simplicity and how alike we all really are. I hope that you will enjoy this book, leaving you with a little smile on your face.

I was encouraged to take my blog and convert it into a book. This was the result of the inspiration and guidance of Russ Gibb, and Dan Stanley, two fine gentlemen from Dearborn, Michigan.

So hang on, and enjoy the ride. I hope it will touch your heart and bring you some joy. ☺

Jennifer Estrada

"Baby's First Word"

Thursday November 17, 2011

Here is my first comic strip on "Jenny's Day", and to be honest, I was more concerned with how I was going to get a hand drawn picture onto the internet rather than drawing it. Anyway, here Is a little story about Jordyn's first word and how she surprised us all.

Jennifer Estrada

"Angel Eye's"

Saturday November 19, 2011

Watching my children grow up and go through stages has really been a learning experience for me. Like I have told Angel, "I was 14 once and I understand, but I have never been the mother of a 14 year old and this is all new to me!" Here is an example of a day living with a teenage girl. It isn't always easy, but it is sometimes very entertaining.

Jenny's Day

"Media is the Message"

Wednesday November 23, 2011

Try explaining to a young boy about presentation and how important it is to make an apology to someone even when you think you have done nothing wrong! Well, this is something that I had to deal with this week with my son Isaiah. Sometimes the way we present something is just as valuable as the act itself. Take a look :)

Jennifer Estrada

"Happy Thanksgiving"

Spending time with the ones we love and creating irreplaceable memories is what life is all about.

Jenny's Day

"A Bug's Life"

Sunday November 29, 2011

Here is a story about my daughter Bella, the sensitive one. A story about life and the realization of how precious a gift that it really is. Enjoy!

Jennifer Estrada

"Never Judge a Book by its Cover"

Thursday December 01, 2011

Having two girls with two completely different personalities isn't always easy. In fact, it hardly ever is. Here is a story about sisterhood and how we should all learn to appreciate each other's differences.

Jenny's Day

"Different Worlds"

Saturday December 03, 2011

No matter how crazy my day gets, and believe me it can get pretty crazy, it's always nice to have somebody to listen to my woes and calmly bring me back down to earth. Unfortunately, that's not always the case :) Take a look.

Jennifer Estrada

"Lions & Tigers & Boots, Oh My!"

Wednesday December 07, 2011

I really enjoy doing stories like this one. It not only shows the ongoing feud between my two lovely daughters, but it also allows me to amplify the importance of a child's imagination. Enjoy!

Jenny's Day

"A Lesson Learned"

Wednesday December 07, 2011

Watching our children struggle is tough for a parent, but watching them learn from their mistakes and succeed makes it all worth-while.

Jennifer Estrada

"Moving Day"

Wednesday December 07, 2011

This week we started the big move into the new house and I thought that I had it all figured out. Aside from the delay of the truck rental, the scratched furniture, and my husband saying "If you want to make an omelet you have to break a few eggs", I learned a few things. . . Always plan for something to go wrong and most of all, if you want something done right, sometimes you have to do it yourself. Check it out.

Jenny's Day

"Star Struck"

Tuesday December 20, 2011

We all have times when we need to be tough, but sometimes we can unknowingly hurt the ones we love. It's good to know when to take off the gear that hides and protects us and just be real. Enjoy :)

Jennifer Estrada

"The Night Before Christmas"

Saturday December 24, 2011

Christmas is such a magical time of year. It's not only a time to give, but is also a time for us to remember our innocence and watch others enjoy theirs. A Merry Christmas to all and to all a good night :)

Jenny's Day

"Reflection"

Wednesday December 28, 2011

We all have moments when we contemplate life and our purpose, *Cogito ergo sum* (I think therefore I am). The answer isn't always clear, but if one would only take a step back they just may see the bigger picture. I titled this "Reflection" not only because of the reflection of thought, but also because I think that we all may see a piece of ourselves glaring back at us. At least I do. Enjoy **:)**

Jennifer Estrada

"Scout Survival"

Thursday December 29, 2011

My son Isaiah has been Boy Scout for many years and let's just say that he has picked up a few skills along the way. Here is an example of one of them. I guess in order to survive in a family of six on a fixed income a boy scout has to do what a boy scout has to do. Enjoy!

Jenny's Day

"A Day in the Life…"

Tuesday January 03, 2012

Since Jordyn has learned to walk I really have had to be on my toes. Everything is a new adventure for her, but I have really enjoyed watching her learn and grow each day as she explores the world around her. Take a look :)

Jennifer Estrada

"Secret Ingredient...Love"

Saturday January 07, 2012

A crush.....boy it can really change a person's outlook on life. Take my daughter Angel for instance. Usually a moody teenager going through the motions and !POW! one cookie from a boy and all is right in the Universe....Take a look!
Oh and Bon Ape'tit :)

Jenny's Day

"The Best of Both Worlds"

Wednesday January 11, 2012

Lately it seems that my husband and I are like two ships passing in the night. One of is either coming or going. And I guess I should be grateful that each of us are employed, but I am even more grateful that our children are provided for and get a little bit of both mom and dad. Take a look :)

Jennifer Estrada

"Growing Pains"

Monday January 16, 2012

This week Bella has been struggling with the possibility that she may be growing up. The mere thought of having to change who she is has been causing her much angst . I just hope that I can make the transition as painless as possible and help her to realize the adventure that lies ahead. Take a look :)

"If growing up means it would be beneath my dignity to climb a tree, I'll never grow up, never grow up, never grow up! Not me!" -Peter Pan

Jenny's Day

"Holy Cow!"

Saturday January 21, 2012

When I was a girl, Sunday was the day that you would get all dressed up and head off to church. Now a days it seems that the most important thing is to "just show up"! Take a look :)

Jennifer Estrada

"Illusions"

Thursday January 26, 2012

Jenny's Day

"Illusions"

Sometimes what we see doesn't always reflect what is truly there. Take my daughters for example...one is at the stage where looks seem to be all that matter, while the other one is trying to grasp the complexity of the day to day thing that we call life. How do you teach your children that physical beauty is fleeting, but what you make of yourself on the inside (inner beauty), that is enduring? Enjoy :)

*"The beauty of a woman is not
in a facial mode
but the true beauty in a woman
is reflected in her soul.
It is the caring that she lovingly gives
the passion that she shows.
The beauty of a woman grows
with the passing years"*

- Audrey Hepburn

Jennifer Estrada

"Ready for Take-Off"

Thursday February 02, 2012

According to the Webster's dictionary, Yo Yo means : a condition or situation marked by regular fluctuations from one extreme to another. This would sum up my Good friend Yolanda to a tee. She is an airline stewardess and while she is traveling the world she picks up interesting facts about the places that she has been and seen. Now only if she would leave some of it in the baggage claim everything would be perfect! Enjoy :)

Jenny's Day

"Violets are Blue"

Monday February 06, 2012

Even when we are aspiring to do some good and maybe even make the world a little better, there may be someone lurking in the shadows waiting for us to fail with their discouragement and doubt. Sometimes it is unintentional and sometimes it is not, but regardless, I believe that is important to never give up on your dreams and to always continue to live life by your standard, not by someone else's.   Enjoy :)

Jennifer Estrada

"Violets are Blue"

"People are often unreasonable, illogical and
self-centered; Forgive them anyway.
If you are kind, people may accuse you of selfish,
ulterior motives; Be kind anyway.
If you are successful, you will win some false friends
and some true enemies; Succeed anyway.
If you are honest and frank, people may cheat you;
Be honest and frank anyway.
What you spend years building, someone could destroy
overnight; Build anyway.
If you find serenity and happiness, they may be jealous;
Be happy anyway.
The good you do today, people will often forget
tomorrow;
Do good anyway.
Give the world the best you have,
and it may never be enough;
Give the world the best you've got anyway.
You see, in the final analysis,
it is between you and God;
It was never between you and them anyway."

~ Mother Theresa

Jenny's Day

"Thank You"

Thursday February 09, 2012

This past week has been very exciting for me! I had the honor of meeting with two lovely ladies from two different local Detroit Newspapers, Katie Hetrick, from the Dearborn Press and Guide, and Marney Rich Keenan, from The Detroit News! Well, to make a long story short, they each did their own story about my blog, Jenny's Day, and the response so far has been wonderful. :) Thank you both, for all of your help!

It's always nice when the ones we love notice all of the little things that we do "because we love them"! Sometimes it is a little too easy to take the people in our life for granted. A simple thank you or I'm sorry may not seem like a lot, but to the people who care, it means the world. This is a little lesson that I tried sharing with my kids recently. I hope that you enjoy :) ....Oh! And thank you for reading.

Jenny's Day

"A Fool for Love"

Thursday February 14, 2012

Happy Valentine's Day! ♥

*"I hold it true, whate'er befall;
I feel it, when I sorrow most;
'Tis better to have loved and lost
Than never to have loved at all."*

~Alfred Lord Tennyson

This week I am trying something new in our household. I am passing on the responsibility of making dinner once a week to the kids. I feel that this will teach them accomplishment and how to contribute more to a group, in this case Family. Let's just hope that they don't burn the house down in the process! We'll see ;)

Jenny's Day

"Food for Thought"

Friday February 24, 2012

Wednesday night dinner with the kids in control........Success!!! To my surprise, with a little help from my "nurturing supervision", the girls did a knock-out job with the evening's spread. They made a Cesar salad followed up with a Shepherd's Pie and Oreo cookie ice-cream for dessert. There were a few entertaining moments throughout the evening, like watching Bella try to chop the onion. She went at it like a killer in a horror film leaving behind mangled fragments of the pungent bulb in her path. And Isaiah, hoping to make us Oreo cookie milk shakes, was unable to find the blender in our still newly moved in to unpacked house.

But after all of that I would definitely have to say how much JOY that it brought me to hear them giggling and laughing through it all. Normally bickering with one another, they found a way to come together, pull it off, and have fun in the process. Now.... seeing how they did such a great job, I am going to make this a weekly routine. :)

"Through all the smiles and trials.....
A family that cooks together....
(along with prayer of course)
Stays together"

Jenny's Day

"House on a Hill"

Jennifer Estrada

"House on a Hill"

*"You are the light of the world.
A town built on a hill cannot be hidden.
Neither do people light a lamp and put it under a bowl.
Instead they put it on its stand,
and it gives light to everyone in the house.
In the same way, let your light shine before others,
that they may see your good deeds
and glorify your Father in heaven."*

~Matthew 5: 14-16

Jenny's Day

"Lookie Lookie"

Thursday March 01, 2012

If you go back a few entries you will see a comic titled, "Secret Ingredient: Love", Angel receiving a cookie from a boy. Let's just say that this is the sequel to that, I'm sure it will reoccur, prologue. Well, it happened, just as we all had assumed, he broke up with her. The attention span of a fifteen year old boy is like that of a monkey in a produce store, grabbing the sweetest ripest fruit in the place and then moving on to the next one! Nevertheless, I think that she handled the whole situation rather well and learned a thing or two about the opposite sex and their disposition in life. As the old saying goes...."That's the way the cookie crumbles!" (I know... it's cheesy)

Jennifer Estrada

"Attention Please"

Thursday March 08, 2012

In our home it seems as though my management of time, or lack thereof, has been an issue of late. The constant battle of who can grab the other's attention in whatever way possible has really been making a lot of noise around here. Among all of my many tasks during the day, the one that is sure to go to the top of the list is to always make sure that the people in my life are my main focus. Everything else will just have to fall into second, or third (or fourth and fifth for that matter).

I would also like to share a message that I received from a Ms. Maria Santiago. It was very encouraging, at a time when I needed it, and it made my heart sing. Thank you for your kind words Maria!

Hi Jennifer!
I am a good friend of Rachel Villanueve-Trejo and went to school with your husband Jesus.

She has been keeping me posted on your exciting story and just yesterday she shared a link to your wonderful accomplishment. I would just like to extend my congratulations to you...it is always great to hear of such a wonderful story. I am very excited and happy for you guys. I have read your blog and I love it...very creative and the humor is right up my alley. I will be sure to purchase your book.

Please send my best to your family!

God Bless & Congratulations!

Jennifer Estrada

"The Luck of the Irish"

Wednesday March 14, 2012

The Blarney Stone : As Irish Legend has it, if one kisses the blue-stone built into the battlements at Blarney Castle, they will receive the gift of gab or eloquence as the story is told. It is said to impart "the ability to deceive without offending." I found this to be an interesting story and I thought that it went right along with my Saint Patrick's Day entry. Now of course there are a few lessons here. First, never talk to strangers who appear suddenly at your window.

Second, don't believe everything your told. And third, there are no such things as Leprechauns. . . .maybe!

♣ Happy St. Patrick's Day! ♣

Wishing you a rainbow

For sunlight after showers—

Miles and miles of Irish smiles

For golden happy hours—

Shamrocks at your doorway

For luck and laughter too,

And a host of friends that never ends

Each day your whole life through!

Jennifer Estrada

"Tennis Anyone?"

Jenny's Day

Tuesday March 20, 2012

As a mother I always try to lead by example and set the pace in my household. Whether or not anyone is paying attention is a whole other affair and with Angel starting Tennis this week at school, I guess that I have had love on my mind. Enjoy :)

A loving heart is the beginning of all knowledge.
~Thomas Carlyle

Jennifer Estrada

"Disregarded Beauty"

Wednesday March 21, 2012

*"For every beauty there is an eye somewhere to see it.
For every truth there is an ear somewhere to hear it.
For every love there is a heart somewhere to receive it"*
~ Ivan Panin

Jenny's Day

"Coming Unplugged"

Panel 1: ISAIAH'S REPORT CARD WASN'T SO GOOD SO I HAD TO TAKE A FEW OF HIS THINGS AWAY AS PUNISHMENT

what'd ya take?

Panel 2: OH JUST HIS VIDEO GAME AND COMPUTER PRIVLAGES UNTIL THE **END** OF THE SCHOOL YEAR

Jennifer Estrada

"Coming Unplugged"

Thursday March 29, 2012

In this day and age it seems as though our children have become part of the "Technological Era". The complaint is no longer "Can I stay outside just a little while longer?" but has now become "I'll go out after I finish this game." They seem to be losing important social skills. Too much is too much and I feel that it is time to pull the plug on our kid's "cyber-displacement" and push them back into reality.

Jenny's Day

"Grande-Osity"

Wednesday April 04, 2012

In case you didn't know, I spend my days in the company of a gentleman by the name of Mr. Russ Gibb, world renowned for burying Paul McCartney of the Beatles on the radio years ago. You see, I help him out throughout the day and little does he know just how much he helps me.

Jennifer Estrada

What he doesn't realize is how nice it is to get out and talk to another adult from time to time, aside from the usual discourse of my children's conversations like, "Can I get a ride" or "What are you making for supper" and "Can't we have something else". It's nice to talk about more sophisticated things even if I do get carried away sometimes. So Thank you Mr. Gibb for all that you do for me and for listening, I think???? You are a cherished friend.

Jenny's Day

"Play Ball"

Thursday April 12, 2012

For weeks I had been wondering why Angel , my oldest teenage daughter who plays on her high school tennis team, was having me pick her up from her practices in the parking lot next to the locker rooms when all of the other girls were being picked up 100 feet away at the tennis courts. And then, watching her strut by the ball field with a very intent glare, I had realized........the baseball team! Oh dear! It's going to be a bumpy ride!

Jennifer Estrada

Every daughter must have an adventure;
she needs to create her own story
to become her own person.

No matter how much mothers,
anxious for their daughters' safety
or success, insist that they "go straight"
to their destination,
daughters must always take
their own circuitous route.

Mothers can only watch and suffer,
or watch and rejoice.

~Josephine Evetts- Secker
Mother and Daughter Tales

Jenny's Day

"Detour Ahead"

Tuesday April 17, 2012

Sometimes the most valuable lessons learned are formed out of chaos. My advice...........learn how to multi-task!!!

*"The road of life twists and turns
and no two directions are ever the same.
Yet our lessons come from the journey,
not the destination."*
~Don Williams Jr.

Jennifer Estrada

"Mother Goose"

Thursday April 19, 2012

Once Upon a Time...

Jenny's Day

As a working mother of four I have a lot of things to remember in one day and well, let's just say that names are not a priority! Enjoy!

OH! I've been told that my dress was a little too high up here! So, I adjusted the amount of leg shown with some editing! Just having fun with this one! :)

Jennifer Estrada

"The most important thing in life is knowing the most important things in life."
~David F. Jakielo

Have Fun!

Jenny's Day

"Stage Left, Right, and Center"

My Husband's Day Off...

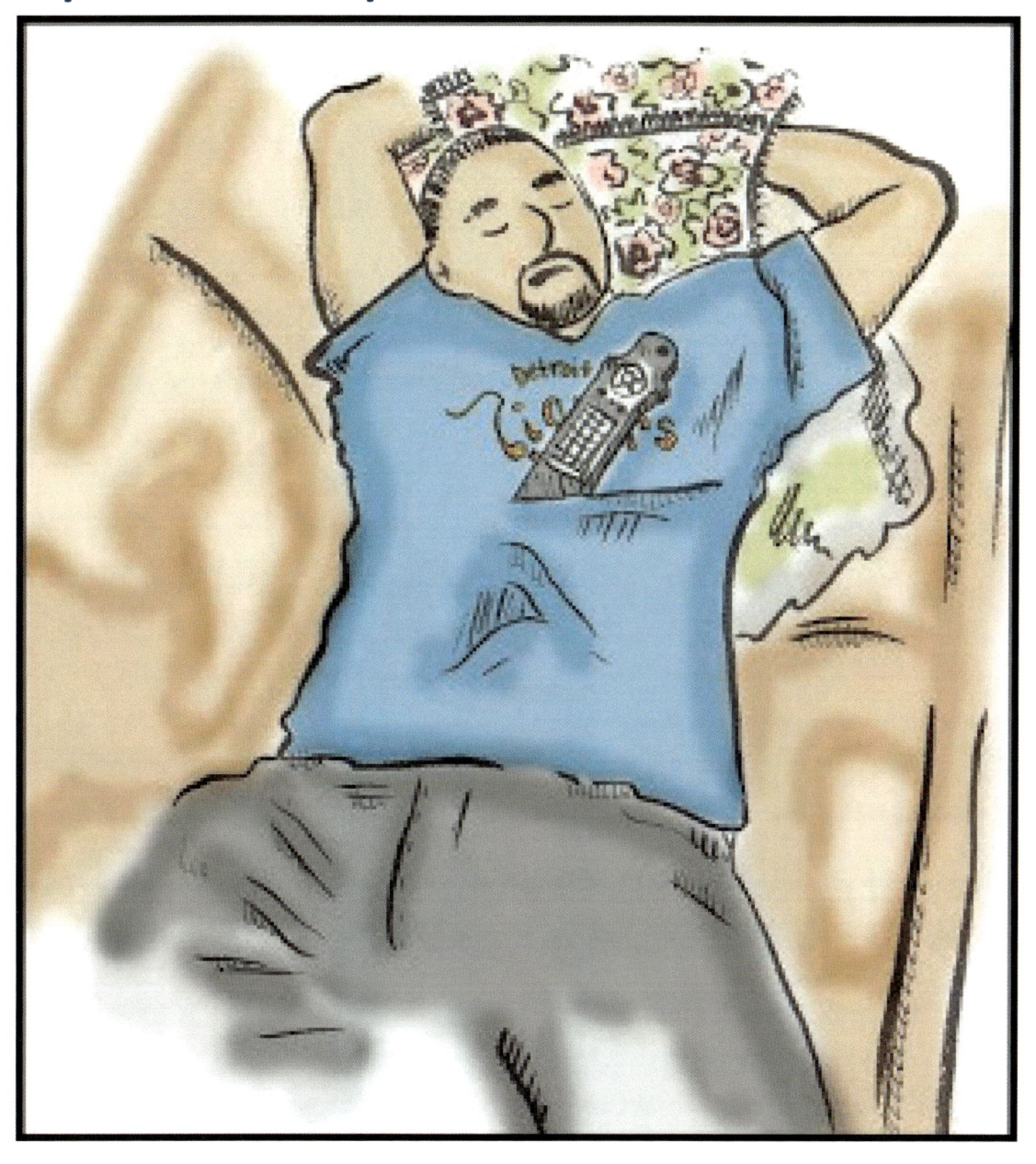

Wednesday April 25, 2012

Literally.

Jennifer Estrada

And Then There's My Day Off!!!

Did I forget to mention nurse, coordinator, counselor, chauffeur, and tutor? Well, I couldn't fit all of that into one picture not to mention my schedule. But I must say that out of all of these, being a mom is by far my favorite role. Enjoy!

"All the world's a stage
And all the men and women merely players
They have their exits and their entrances
And one man [or woman] in his time plays many parts"
~William Shakespeare

Jenny's Day

"Income-ing Breaking News!"

Wednesday May 02, 2012

The past few weeks have been quite interesting to say the least. Do you have a moment? Sit down and I'll tell you about it. As some of you may know my husband and I share the responsibilities of both working, paying the bills, and parenting our four growing children. My husband has recently returned to his old profession, roofing, and with all of the rain here in Michigan of late, he has not been working as much as we had hoped. This led to some cuts in the budget putting our cable and internet services onto the chopping board. Like I told the kids, "You can't eat television!"

Jennifer Estrada

*"Oh why don't you save
all the money you earn?
Well if I didn't eat,
I'd have money to burn."*
~ Harry Mac McClintock

Hallejuah I'm A Bum!

Jenny's Day

"Uphill"

This Road Is Bumpy
My Feet Are Soar
My Body Is Aching
I Can't Take Anymore
I Keep On Drudging
For Other's Sake
For Their Own Happiness
A Smile I Fake
A Heart So Full Of Love
For All Those Around
I Will Keep Forever Searching
For Some Kind And Calmer Ground
It Is An Uphill Battle
A Fight I Plan To Keep
Until I Find Life's Answers
For This Is What I Seek

~Jennifer Estrada
2/11/2011

Monday May 07, 2012

"Sometimes the path you're on is not as important as the direction you're heading."
~Kevin Smith

Jennifer Estrada

"Keep Your Eye On The Ball"

Thursday May 10, 2012

Isabella has the passion to become many things and it has recently come to my attention that one of her countless conquests is to become "the President of the United States". "That's a pretty big goal", I said. "But if you focus, you can do anything that you put your mind to.

Jenny's Day

Just don't do too many things at once!" Someone once said, "If you chase two rabbits they will both get away!"

"All men dream: but not equally.
Those who dream by night
in the dusty recesses of their minds
wake in the day to find
that it was vanity:
but the dreamers of the day
are dangerous men,
for they may act their dream
with open eyes,
to make it possible."

~T.E. Lawrence,
Seven Pillars of Wisdom, 1926

Jennifer Estrada

"A Mother's Love"

I lost you 25 years ago to cancer, and I will never forget

your kindness, your struggle, your strength

But the greatest lesson that you had ever taught me in life, was to love.

I love you Mom ♥

RIP
5/31/87

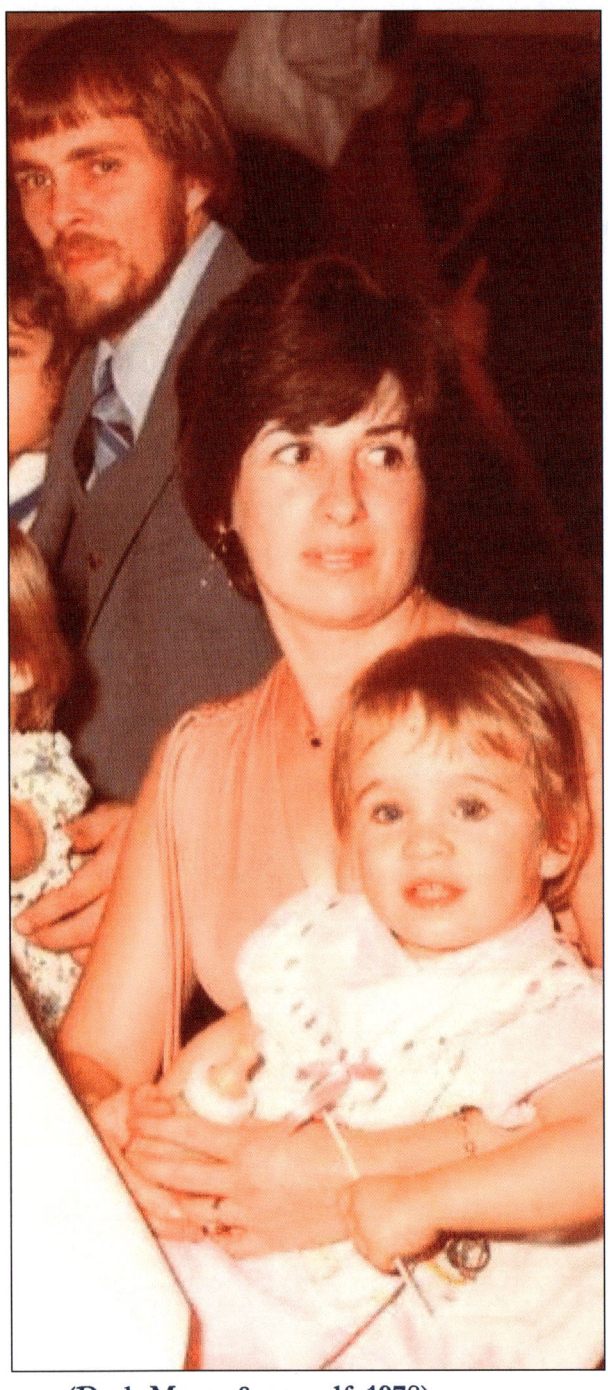

(Dad, Mom, & myself, 1978)

"Character 101"

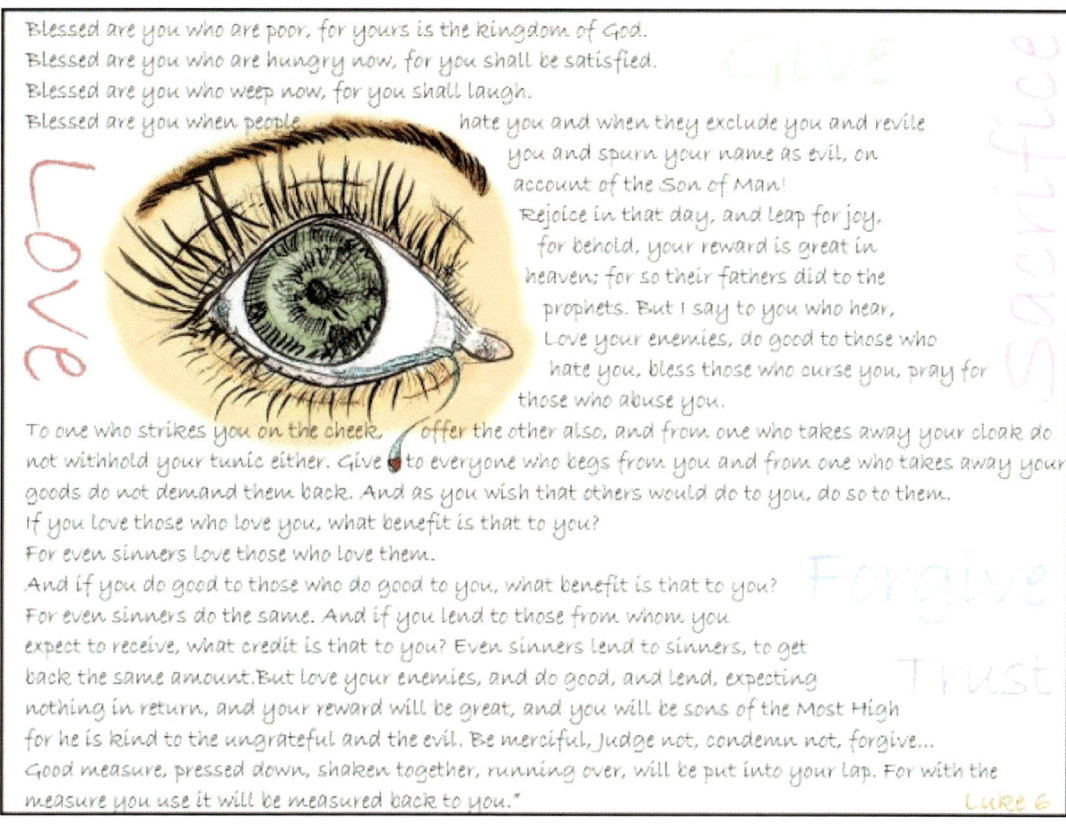

> Blessed are you who are poor, for yours is the kingdom of God.
> Blessed are you who are hungry now, for you shall be satisfied.
> Blessed are you who weep now, for you shall laugh.
> Blessed are you when people hate you and when they exclude you and revile you and spurn your name as evil, on account of the Son of Man!
> Rejoice in that day, and leap for joy, for behold, your reward is great in heaven; for so their fathers did to the prophets. But I say to you who hear, Love your enemies, do good to those who hate you, bless those who curse you, pray for those who abuse you.
> To one who strikes you on the cheek, offer the other also, and from one who takes away your cloak do not withhold your tunic either. Give to everyone who begs from you and from one who takes away your goods do not demand them back. And as you wish that others would do to you, do so to them.
> If you love those who love you, what benefit is that to you?
> For even sinners love those who love them.
> And if you do good to those who do good to you, what benefit is that to you?
> For even sinners do the same. And if you lend to those from whom you expect to receive, what credit is that to you? Even sinners lend to sinners, to get back the same amount. But love your enemies, and do good, and lend, expecting nothing in return, and your reward will be great, and you will be sons of the Most High for he is kind to the ungrateful and the evil. Be merciful, judge not, condemn not, forgive... Good measure, pressed down, shaken together, running over, will be put into your lap. For with the measure you use it will be measured back to you."
>
> Luke 6

Love · Give · Sacrifice · Forgive · Trust

Friday May 18, 2012

Instead of a lesson for the children, this week I felt that it t'was I who needed a refresher course in character. Even we parents need a reminder from time to time to help keep us on track and I just so happened to stumble upon the book of Luke, chapter 6:27-38, and what perfect timing.

Jennifer Estrada

Her eyes are homes of silent prayers.
~Alfred Tennyson.

___

This is the precious present
regardless of what yesterday was like
regardless of what tomorrow may bring.
When your inner eyes open
you can find immense beauty hidden within the
inconsequential details of daily life.
When your inner ears open
you can hear the subtle, lovely
music of the universe everywhere you go.
When the heart of your heart opens
you can take deep pleasure in the company
of the people around you...
family, friends, acquaintances, or strangers
including those whose characters are less than perfect
just as your character is less than perfect.
When you are open to the beauty, mystery, and grandeur
of ordinary existence, you "get it"
that it always has been beautiful, mysterious,
and grand and always will be.
This is the precious present.
~Timothy Ray Miller

Jenny's Day

"Happy Memorial Day"

KIDS... IT'S TIME TO PUT UP THE FLAG!

YOU MAY NOT BE ALLOWED TO IN SCHOOL... BUT AT HOME WE WILL SAY THE PLEDGE OF ALLEGIANCE! WHERE IS BELLA?

Bella!

HERE SHE COMES

I'M READY!!!

Monday May 28, 2012

Jennifer Estrada

Patriotism, as defined by our Webster's Dictionary, is the devoted love, support, and defense of one's country; an absolute loyalty. When I was young this was taught to us not only in school, but also at home. I can still remember my father taking us outside to hang up the flag and with my mother, coming to the United States as a little girl and later on becoming a citizen, saying that no matter what we were without we were always blessed just to have been born here. With that being said I feel that it is our responsibility as parents to do the same.

And may God Bless America and our troops!

I pledge allegiance to the flag,
of the United States of America,
And to the republic for which it stands,
One nation, under God, indivisible, with liberty and justice for all.

Jenny's Day

"Happy Birthday"

Thursday June 07, 2012

O.K.....So I'm not like your average mom. Most mother's would love a day at the spa, a bouquet of flowers, or maybe even a shiny new ring. Not me! I like tools! Anything that will cut my work time in half and makes my life a bit easier so that I can enjoy the people in my life is fine by me. Thank you (my family) for such a wonderful birthday!

Jennifer Estrada

"Dost thou love life?
Then do not squander time,
for that is the stuff life is made of."
- Benjamin Franklin.

Jenny's Day

"Sugar & Spice"

Tuesday June 19, 2012

"Sugar and Spice and everything nice, that's what little girls are made of" or that's what they say anyway until they hit the age of about fifteen and then it's more like salt and vinegar!

Jennifer Estrada

Today Angel needed a little reminder about how things work around here like who puts the food in front of her, the roof over her head, and hopefully she learned to be careful of what you wish for because your wish just might actually come true. Oh... I did eventually let her back in.....eventually :)

> *"People who bite the hand*
> *that feeds them*
> *usually lick the boot*
> *that kicks them."*
> ~Eric Hoffer

Jenny's Day

"The Laws of Motion"

The three laws of motion rendered to us by the great Sir Isaac Newton can be applied to life in so many ways and are as follows:

1. An object at rest will remain at rest unless acted on by an unbalanced force.

2. Acceleration is produced when a force acts on a mass.

Monday June 25, 2012

Jennifer Estrada

And finally....

3. For every action there is an equal and opposite reaction!

Having to deal with the ongoing battle of my bickering brood, I have noticed that Bella in particular, has been forming a rebellion against her older sister's derision. Now if I could only teach her to use her powers for good instead of evil we'll be good to go!

Enough said.....

WHEN YOU PUSH AN OBJECT, IT PUSHES BACK.

Jenny's Day

"Garden Philosophy"

Wednesday June 27, 2012

Just when I think that I am about to have a meaningful conversation with my son...well you know what happened. What I was going to say is that life is a lot like a garden because one must invest an effort into making it beautiful. And if the garden just so happens to be neglected, with the right tools and some extra work, it can be made beautiful again

Jennifer Estrada

"Kiss of the sun for pardon.
Song of the birds for mirth.
You're closer to God's heart in a garden
than any place else on earth."
~Dorothy Frances Gurney

"Life is like a garden...dig it!"
~Joe Dirt

Jenny's Day

"When The Cat's Away...

Tuesday July 10, 2012

...the mice will play!"

Jennifer Estrada

"My Story"

I know that it has been awhile since my last entry, but for some hounding reason I felt that on this one I would take my time and attempt to inject a bit more honesty into my drawings. With the understanding of how vulnerable this might make me, I decided to go along with my instincts, and I must say that I am quite pleased with the result. So take it or leave it, here it goes......

You know how in most comics the hero usually has this one defining moment in their life that changes everything? That one event that sets them on the path to their inevitable destiny?

Jenny's Day

For example...

SPIDER BITE	BORN A MUTANT	GAIN VAST INTELLECT
FIND MJOLNIR	PARENTS DEATH	GAMMA RADIATION
BUILD METAL SUIT	LEARN MAGIC	LAB DISASTER
COSMIC RAYS	WEAR ALIEN SYMBIOTE	GOVERNMENT TESTING

(Artist Unknown)

Jennifer Estrada

Well, this is a brief narration of that moment, or moments, in my life. This is my story.

MY LIFE STARTED OUT LIKE MANY OTHER'S, IN A FAMLY...

SURROUNDED BY... LOVE

THAT I WAS DIFFERENT! WHILE OTHER GIRLS WERE WORRIED ABOUT WHAT TO WEAR...I WAS CONTEMPLATING LIFE & DEATH

AND THEN THAT FATEFUL DAY ARRIVED...

THE DAY I LOST MY MOM. THE DAY THAT I HAD REALIZED...

HOWL

AS FAR AS I COULD TELL EVERY CARNG ADULT IN MY LIFE HAD FALLEN OFF OF THE PLANET. NOT AN AUNT, AN UNCLE OR EVEN A SOCIAL WORKER HAD ARRIVED. MY INNOCENCE WAS GONE AND MY BURDON WAS HANDED TO ME. I FELT **ALONE**

AMBULANCE 911

AND JUST WHEN I THOUGHT THINGS COULDN'T GET ANY WORSE, MY FATHER WAS RUSHED AWAY NEVER TO RETURN, FALLING VICTIM TO HIS POOR HEALTH...

Jenny's Day

Monday July 23, 2012

"When I was 5 years old, my mother always told me
that happiness was the key to life.
When I went to school,
they asked me what I wanted to be when I grew up.
I wrote down 'happy.'
They told me I didn't understand the assignment,
and I told them they didn't understand life."
- John Lennon

Jennifer Estrada

"Don't Give Up!"

Jenny's Day

Monday August 20, 2012

Many times people give up too soon surrendering to the pain completely unaware of how close that they really were to accomplishing their goal.

While waiting for my Chinese take-out with the girls, I challenged them to an arm-wrestling competition. With the girls both being lefties I chose to use my (weaker) left arm as well.

The match ensued and my arm was killing me. And just when I thought that they were going to win...they quit! So my lesson here is to never give up, push through the pain, and take the victory!

Jennifer Estrada

***"The greatest oak
was once a little nut who held its
ground."***
~Author Unknown

Jenny's Day

"I am a Soldier"

Monday September 10, 2012

In addition to all this, take up the shield of faith, with which you can extinguish all the flaming arrows of the evil one. Take the helmet of salvation and the sword of the Spirit, which is the word of God And pray in the Spirit on all occasions with all kinds of prayers and requests. With this in mind, be alert and always keep on praying for all the Lord's people.
~Ephesians 6:16-18

I Am A Soldier
"I am a soldier in the army of my God. The Lord Jesus Christ is my commanding officer. The Holy Bible is my code of conduct. Faith, prayer, and the Word are my weapons of warfare.
I have been taught by the Holy Spirit, trained by experience, tried by adversity and tested by fire.

I am a volunteer in this army, and I am enlisted for eternity. I will either retire in this army at the Rapture or die in this army; but I will not get out, sell out, be talked out, or pushed out.
I am faithful, reliable, capable and dependable. If my God needs me, I am there. If He needs me in the Sunday school, to teach the children, work with the youth, help adults or just sit and learn, He can use me because I am there!

I Am A Soldier
I am not a baby. I do not need to be pampered, petted, primed up, pumped up, picked up or pepped up.

Jenny's Day

I Am A Soldier

No one has to call me, remind me, write me, visit me, entice me, or lure me.

I Am A Soldier

I am not a wimp. I am in place, saluting my King, obeying His orders, praising His name, and building His kingdom! No one has to send me flowers, gifts, food, cards, candy or give me handouts. I do not need to be cuddled, cradled, cared for, or catered to. I am committed. I cannot have my feelings hurt bad enough to turn me around. I cannot be discouraged enough to turn me aside. I cannot lose enough to cause me to quit.

When Jesus called me into this army, I had nothing. If I end up with nothing, I will still come out ahead. I will win. My God has and will continue to supply all of my needs. I am more than a conqueror. I will always triumph. I can do all things through Christ. Devils cannot defeat me. People cannot disillusion me. Weather cannot weary me. Sickness cannot stop me. Battles cannot beat me. Money cannot buy me. Governments cannot silence me and hell cannot handle me.

I Am A Soldier

Even death cannot destroy me. For when my commander calls me from this battlefield, He will promote me to Captain and then allow me to rule with Him.

Jennifer Estrada

I am a soldier in the army, and I'm marching claiming victory. I will not give up. I will not turn around.

I am a soldier, marching heaven bound. Here I stand! Will you stand with me?"

~Pastor Cindye Coates M.Div.

Jenny's Day

"The Simplicity of a Flower"

"The Simplicity of a Flower"
Growing in a field
The Simplicity of a Flower
To Earthly Seasons yield
Its secrets hold much power
Protected as a bud
Its petals not yet seen
And with maturity opens
Outstretched
Looking
Yearning
Reaching for the sun
But what lies beneath the green?
Forget life's complications
sit
And just be still
Let go of the pain
And take in the rain
For soon the storm will pass
Dark clouds are fading
Sun now cascading
Consume the light
Collect the rays
As do the chloroplasts
And only when
Young bloom then opens
Do we really see what's true
The beauty
The colors
The wonder
The fading
To be replaced by
something new

Sunday November 25, 2012

Jennifer Estrada

"Who's Afraid of the Big Bad Wolf"

Thursday December 06, 2012

The Big Bad Wolf & Little Red Riding Hood featuring The Three Blind Mice. (created by Mrs. Jennifer Estrada)

Many times we go about our daily lives with good intentions, attempting to help out our fellow man. But our day to day benevolence doesn't always come with a warning label!

Jenny's Day

In fact, we on occasion can become blinded by our conscience and moral cultivation. Sometimes situations, or people for that matter, aren't always as they seem.

Einstein was once quoted saying, "If you want your children to be intelligent, read them fairy tales. If you want them to be even more intelligent, read them more fairy tales." I have never found this to be more true as I do now that I am an adult. You can learn a lot from a little old fairy tale and a big dose of good old fashion common sense. In some situations we have to take off our rose colored glasses and take heed to the wolves in sheep's clothing!

"Watch out for false prophets.
They come to you in sheep's clothing,
but inwardly they are ferocious wolves.
~Matthew 7:15

Jennifer Estrada

Did you know the origin of the 'tale' of the Three Blind Mice?

The origin of the words to the Three Blind Mice rhyme are based in English history. The 'farmer's wife' refers to the daughter of King Henry VIII, Queen Mary I. Mary was a staunch Catholic and her violent persecution of Protestants led to the nickname of 'Bloody Mary'. The reference to 'farmer's wife' in Three blind mice refers to the massive estates which she, and her husband King Philip of Spain, possessed.

The 'three blind mice' were three noblemen who adhered to the Protestant faith and who were convicted of plotting against the Queen - she did not have them dismembered and blinded as inferred in Three Blind Mice, but she did have them burnt at the stake!

Jenny's Day

"Silver and Gold"

FATHER...WHY DO WE GIVE PRESENTS ON CHRISTMAS?

Sunday December 23, 2012

Jennifer Estrada

"GO CHILD AND SEE, THE VERY FIRST GIFT OF CHRISTMAS..."

Jenny's Day

...THE MOST PRECIOUS PRESENT OF ALL!

Above: 26 stars of remembrance for those who lost their lives in Newtown, CT. Thanks to my beautiful daughter Isabella for helping me with some of the graphics! I love you!

Children.
Isn't that what Christmas is all about? To try to give them the same joy on Christmas morning that they give to us all year? A magical time to return the smiles that they give to us and to see their shining faces as they open each present one by one?

Jennifer Estrada

And it all started with the very first gift of Christmas...

A child more precious than silver or gold!
Our children, the greatest treasure
that God can bestow.
Who love us unconditionally both day and night.
A reward unto itself when We hold Them tight.
That glimmer of innocence in their eyes.
The pain we feel when we hear them cry.
So hold them close and teach them well.
For the value of a child is a gift,
not one can tell.
~Mrs. Jennifer Estrada

Have a Blessed and Very Merry Christmas!

Thank you for purchasing my book and allowing our family to share a small glimpse of our family life. Stay tuned for future editions of my drawings, words of wisdom and mother love both on my website, www.jennysday.com, as well as in paperback form. It has been a pleasure to open our world and share it with others.

Jenny

Jennifer Estrada

JENNY'S DAY
www.jennysday.com

Please enjoy some of the comments from my website subscribers.

Jenny Estrada demonstrates marvelous ability in her drawings while capturing those delightful moments between mother and child that are an important part of growing up. Good stuff, Jenny and thanks Russellbob for sharing it with us.
--by Jim D

"Jenny's Day" is very sweet and well done. It's important to write about what you know best. Jennifer's experiences as a Mom should strike a chord with a very large common audience.
--by Leo

Jenny's Day is a delight. Bella is already my favorite her love of "bug people" captured my heart.
by Jake S

Jenny's Day' is fun! Congratulations to Ms. Estrada!
--by Dearborn Observer